I'M NOT

A GOOD GIRL

FIRST BOOK OF THE SERIES

GOOD GIRLS WRITE POETRY

Aurora June

Contents

About The Author

Aurora is a Portuguese young lawyer from Portugal.

She loves to read romances and non-fiction books.

She's a cat person and a coffee lover. She's fascinated by romance, drama, spicy and twists.

Her debut novel is "All Kinds of Wrong", the first of the series "The New Romantics".

You can find more about the author by following her on Instagram @aurorajuneauthor

Dedication

To all the girls who feel obligated to be good girls instead of doing whatever the hell they want to.

Good Girls Don't…

Good Girls don't bother

Good Girls don't fight

Good Girls don't shout out

Good Girls don't cry

Good Girls wait for you to call

Good Girls never make the first move

Good Girls never say it's your fault

To them, there's nothing you need to prove

But Good Girls are so boring

Because they don't even exist

If you meet one, just run

There's a good chance she's twisted.

Who wants to be a good girl, anyway?

There's no place for them in the world.

There's a big chance they'll end up married

with a small dick and

caged like a bird.

Too

Her skirt is too short

Her cleavage is too open

Her lips are too red

Her fabric is too tight.

Her eyes are demanding

Her manners are too rough

Her words are too dirty

Her curses are too huff

She scares you, doesn't she?

She's unlike any other girls.

She's special and,

You're not gonna conquer her with pearls.

You won't be able to boss her around,

You're not gonna change her.

Don't you try to corner her,

That way, you're gonna lose her.

Show her your respect,

Show that you accept her,

Be a truly partner,

Be worthy of her.

Because,

She's not too anything,

She's the perfect amount.

I Hate It

Boy, I hate it when you're right.

I hate it when you're wrong

I hate it when we fight.

I hate when it's my fault.

I hate when you're not at home

I hate it when I'm all alone

I hate it when you leave upset

I hate that we might be done.

I know I'm stubborn, I hate it

I know I'm selfish, I hate it

I know I'm needy, I hate it.

I know I love you too much

I hate it.

But the truth is

I rather fight you every day at home

I rather hate it,

Than love you without having you at all.

I'm All Flavors

I am salty.

I'm spicy.

I'm sweet.

I'm all flavors.

You may think it's too much.

But life would be tasteless

without me.

I mean, there's always a risk in spicy food.

You can run out of air.

You can even choke.

You can cry because it's too much.

So…

Admit it.

You love me salty.

You love me spicy.

You love me sweet.

Baby, Please Don't Go

Baby, please don't go

Can't you see how good we are together?

Let's kiss and make love

Let's smile

Let's dance in the rain

Let's make fun of everyone

Let's make promises

Let's make plans

Let's plan trips

Let's make babies

Baby, please don't go

There are so many words I want to say

So many promises I want to keep

So many babies I want to make with you.

Baby, just come home

Come to bed.

Or let's go outside

And dance in the rain.

Let's cook together

And laugh about how bad it is.

And then, let's order some food.

Can't you see, baby?

I'm happy

As long as I'm with you.

So…

Even if there's no rain so we can dance

Even if you're too tired to make love

Even if we can't keep our promises.

Baby, please don't go

Can't you see how good we are together?

Haters Gonna Hate

Darling, come on!

You can't please everyone.

Don't try too hard,

They're not even worth it.

Haters gonna hate,

No matter what you do,

So wear whatever you want,

Don't wait for their review.

Because people are mean,

They'll talk about you,

Whether you wear red or black,

They'll gossip about you.

Don't worry, it's not your fault,

Sad people become haters,

They can't deal with other's happiness,

So they become dictators.

Haters gonna hate,

So don't try too hard.

They'll just hate you more

You can't please everyone.

I Wish I Was Yours

Oh, I wish I was yours.

Yours to take

Yours to love

Yours to praise.

I wish you said

You're only mine

I wish you would take me at night

In the dark,

When nobody is awake.

Claiming me.

Holding me.

Loving me.

I wish you were jealous of me.

I wish you hated the men around me

Those who look at me

Wishing I was theirs.

But no.

You don't claim me

You don't take me at night

You don't want me to be yours.

You don't even see me.

But I wish so bad that I was yours.

Between Love and Hate

Everyone says that

There's a fine line

Between love and hate.

Is it truth?

I mean,

When you make fun of me

When you curse my clothes

When you look at me angry.

There's no way this is love.

Right?

But then…

You curse all the other boys

You make them stay away

You watch it when I dance

You look for me every day.

When I smile, you make me cry.

But when I cry, you make stop.

When I go to parties

You make me leave

Only so you can run after me.

You always say I'm so different than other
girls

Is that a good thing

or a bad thing?

I wish I knew, because

Love or hate

It's burning.

I see it in your eyes, you know?

The way you hate yourself,

Because you want me.

The way you hate me,

Because you want me.

There's a fine line

Between love and hate.

And baby… I love you too.

To Love Only One Boy

Who said

I had to choose only one?

I mean,

Life is too short

The world is too big

Things are too messy,

To love only one boy.

There are too many parties

The sunset is too pretty

The sea is too salty,

To love only one boy.

The nights are too hot

The days are too big

The drinks are too strong,

To love only one boy.

And there are so many handsome boys

There are so many sweet boys

To love only one boy.

I mean,

How would I choose, anyway?

There are so many summer nights.

So many books to read.

So many dives to take.

To love only one boy.

Wild Girl

There's this girl

who grew up in the countryside.

Maybe you've never seen her,

because she likes to hide.

She's like a ghost, they say

But they are wrong.

She just never goes

Where she doesn't belong.

Because the truth about this girl…

She's unpredictable

She's strong

She's irresistible

She has a mind of her own.

She doesn't like to be stuck.

She can't be tied.

She doesn't like cages

Her freedom is her pride.

So don't try to hold her,

Don't scare her

Or she'll run away

She's not a ghost

But she can turn into one,

If someone makes her stay.

You're Not The Boss Of Me

You're not the boss of me.

Did you know that?

I'm a girl with a mind of my own.

So believe me

When I tell you that…

Loving you is a choice,

Not an inevitability.

Do you know why?

Even if my heart loves you

Even if my body burns for you

I'm the one who calls the shots.

Baby, I could love you

All night

Without wanting you.

Because I'm a girl with a mind of my own.

So don't you think, even for a second

That my love for you

Is a curse.

Because even if I love you with all my heart

My love is a choice

Not a curse.

I'm a girl with a mind of my own,

And you're not the boss of me.

You Want Me So Bad, Pretty Boy

I know you want me,

Am I right?

Oh, you want me so bad.

When I pass by your side,

When I dance with other boys

When I laugh to their jokes

When I pretend, I'm having fun.

While you kiss your girlfriend

While I kiss my boyfriend

While we fuck in his bedroom

Oh, you want me so bad.

It's okay, pretty boy

I won't tell

It's our dirty little secret.

That you kiss her,

Thinking of me.

That you text him, your best friend

While you touch me.

They can't find out

It would be tragic.

And we both know that

You want me so so bad

Because it's our dirty little secret.

The Breakup Poem

I'm sorry, baby

But this isn't working.

I wish I could say

It's not you, it's me,

But I would be lying.

Because the truth, baby,

Is that

It is you.

Of course it's you.

You're boring

You're selfish

You're snob

You're vanish.

You are mean to people.

You are dumb as a stone

You brag about your parents' money

Really, I'm better on my own.

Besides,

Your haircut looks so tacky

I wanted to tell you for some time

I heard the same from Jackie

From behind it looks like a climb.

So I guess we should break up

It's not like it was true love

If it was to you, I'm really sorry

But we don't even have a song.

My First Kiss

My first kiss was perfect,
Perfectly ridiculous.

I was thirteen and in love
By the cutest boy in school
All the other girls wanted him
But I was the biggest fool.

You see,
He was a dork
But at thirteen I was dumb
Thank God, he moved to New York
He was always chewing that stupid gum.

The kiss was a disaster,

He took me by surprise

He stuck his tongue down my throat

Needless to say, I punched his eye.

And that wasn't even the worst.

God, I was so dumb.

So when he tried to eat my mouth,

I swallowed his gum.

I'm Not A Writer

I'm not a writer

I'm a dreamer

I dream of a world that doesn't exist

And with characters not yet born.

So I try to put it on paper

And sometimes I screw it up.

I keep thinking, I'm gonna make it

Right before I slump.

It's not easy to be a writer

Even if you're not a writer at all

You put all these words on paper

And then you throw your computer against
the wall.

The Fucking Cheater

Don't call me anymore,

I already blocked you

I already told you before

I don't get fooled twice.

I knew something was wrong,

You were always so late

And the little dummy home alone

Making the dinner you never ate

It's not like I loved you that much,

But I hate being lied to.

On top of that she's uglier than me

Come on, she was the best you could do?

My friends always said you were sassy.
But I didn't want to believe it.
Maybe you'll cheat longer next time
Good luck to that girl, she's gonna need it.

A cheater is always a cheater
Until the cheater gets cheated.
I swear, I would love to see your face
Seeing the pics of your friend doing me.

We End Up Having Sex

Baby, I'm bored.

We've done this a thousand times

You want to break up? Let's do it.

Just don't come crawl to me next time.

Because I agree with you,

We're a mess.

Always fighting for nothing

Or having sex.

It's too hard,

I can't do it anymore.

Just find someone else to bother

My knees are sore from rubbing the floor.

You forget our birthday, we fight

And we end up having sex.

I come home late, we fight,

We end up having sex.

It's not ideal and I'm not that horny,

But after a fight, it feels good to feel your
cock

But then you come in like ten seconds

And you fell asleep as a rock.

So to make it better

We should break up

Over the phone, if it's possible.

So we don't end up having sex.

Look Up, My Eyes Are Up Here

Look up, perv

My eyes are up here.

A cleavage is not an invitation.

My eyes are up here.

In case no one has told you,

When you talk to someone, you look them
in the eye

My tits are not part of my face

My eyes are up here, perv.

When you talk to men,

You also look at their chests?

I'd like to see that, perv

Maybe we should do that test.

I wear cleavage so I feel pretty.

But not pretty for you, perv.

I dress for myself, to please myself.

So don't look at what doesn't belong to you.

My eyes are up here, perv.

Look me in the eyes

Be a man, lift your head

You might find a surprise.

Because,

My eyes are up here.

Rich Girls

Soft skin

Straight hair

White teeth

Branded clothing.

They're rich girls.

It comes natural to them.

Elegance and Class

Style and Power.

It sounds so simple,

So fucking perfect.

Can't they get a disgusting pimple?

Get their faces a little wrecked?

Oh, I know, I'm being unfair
It's not their fault they got it all
Poor girls, they have problems too
Good luck to you, if you become one.

I'm kidding, I have pimples too
Sometimes my hair has crawls
It's okay, I can get it fixed.
I'm a rich girl, after all.

Maybe I'm Not The Protagonist

I've been reading novels since I was
thirteen.

I always dreamed with my story of love,

But now, I'm almost thirty,

And the story hasn't even begun.

I start thinking I'm not the protagonist.

That in this book, I have a secondary role.

Shit, maybe I'm the best friend or the
doorman,

Please, not the doorman!

My feet are always so cold.

Or maybe, I really am the protagonist

And this book is just a bad one.

If it's that, maybe there will be a twist

Where I end up dead or I fall in love.

I'm Frisky

Hi gorgeous,

Never seen you here before.

Stay around, lets hang out

Maybe some action on the floor.

They say I'm frisky,

They don't even know

Don't believe what they say,

Because it's three times more.

I'll take care of you

I promise you a good time

So you choose:

Your place or mine?

That's right, I don't wait around

For men who don't know what they want

If I want something, I go get it

Right now, it's you who I want.

But don't flatter yourself, I'm unpredictable

I might not want you for long

So enjoy this ride while you can

You might improve your chances with your
tongue.

The truth is, I'm just a girl

And girls just wanna have fun

Kiss me, spoil me, make me dirty

Enjoy the ride, gorgeous

It's you who I want.

Burned Down A Church

They call me crazy

I think it's too much

It wasn't so bad, you know? They're
overreacting

I only burned down a church.

It wasn't my fault, you know? I swear,

I didn't want everything to burn.

But when the old ladies started whispering

I knew something had to be done.

I lit a match, no one saw me

And I took the flame to the old lady's skirt

But the old lady didn't notice

One minute later it was on her shirt

They were whispering so they didn't notice
And who am I to interrupt?
Only when their ass started to burn,
They finally got up.

It was too funny, so I started to laugh.
Maybe that was my mistake
Because they freaked out and called the
cops,
They called me crazy and put me in jail.

They got me handcuffed like a mental
But I'm not crazy, I'm just bold

That's what I'll tell the judge
Or I'll burn down the court.

I'll Be Your Fucking Nightmare

You played me like a fool,
So deluded in your scheme.
I believed in you, look where it took me
Nothing is never what it seems.

I admit, I was too easy
So proud that you'd chosen me.
That little girl was ridiculous
But now I'll be a fucking queen.

Don't worry, you'll get to see me
I'll appear in your fucking dreams
I'll be there when you least expect me,
Nothing is never what it seems.

Baby, I promise you one thing,

The good girl became the devil,

You ruined all my sweet dreams?

I'll become your fucking nightmare.

That Look On Your Face

Baby I would give anything

To see that look on your face.

The one you give me when your first saw
me

On my wet white dress with a lace.

Until you got your way, you were a like
stalker

You called, you smiled, you chased.

You didn't give up until you had me

That look always on your face.

One night, I agreed to meet you

In the back seat of your car

You lifted my dress and I moaned,

And you realized you had already won.

I took off my panties and your dick
throbbed

That look always on your face

You put the condom, I spread my legs

And then it was like a race.

One minute and it was over,

I didn't even come.

Over was also that look

That look on your face.

I've Been There, Honey

I've been there, honey,

Don't recommend it.

But you look like you won a lot of money.

Let me tell you, honey

He's not that good.

He does it so bad,

It's not even funny.

Right now, you may be blind

Because he's good at the eyes

But coming before the girl is just unkind

Don't let him tell you otherwise.

He won't know how to find your clit

He'll ask you if you can help
Whatever you do don't let him finger you,
Or there will be some yelp.

But the worst of it is his tongue
Just thinking of it makes me whimper
I almost lost my lung
Because I couldn't stop screaming.

And not in a good way, I swear
Don't let his tongue come near you.
He will dig you up like a lizard
He doesn't even have a clue.

I've been there honey, I've done that
So run away while you can
He's not even a good kisser,
Search better, you'll find a man.

I Did Something Bad

Ups baby, I did something bad

It wasn't on purpose, I swear

I was an accident,

But I don't really care.

You know I'm cranky

And you hurt my feelings

What did you expect?

I had to do something

It was my healing

And I also made a bet.

So, your friend was there

And I was lonely

And he's so hot

And he came bare.

It was one time only
On your couch
Don't worry,
Your dad wasn't there.

Next time, you think better
When you try to contradict me
You know I'm cranky, it's not my fault
Just don't try to trick me.

Because baby, you have more friends
And I heard they like to share
But don't worry, I'll be good
As long as you stop fucking Blair.

My Friend' Boyfriends

They're perfect, they're untouchable

A chivalry that never ends

They hot, smart and rich

They're my friend' boyfriends

The best boyfriends in the world

Never forget a birthday

Every day they buy them flowers

Every day they make my day

They're concerned and attentive

They don't mind going shopping

They prepare surprises

They're just the perfect boyfriends.

But my friends don't know their luck

They are always complaining

Because their friend' boyfriends

Are the most entertaining

You're never happy with what you want

Cause your friend' toys always seem better

So shut up and spoil your boyfriend

While he's making your friends wetter.

My Dad Never Liked You

My dad never liked you

He used to tell me all the time

He said you were a pussy

I guess he was right.

I should've seen the signs

They were all there

I guess I was to blind

But my dad was aware.

He said you didn't have it,

That you were as useless as your hair,

You were nice to look at

But didn't have anything to add.

So you were right when you said he didn't
like you

I just lied so you wouldn't feel bad.

Your attempts to change it were pathetic

At least when we broke up, we was glad.

Marry Me

Baby, let's get married this weekend

I know it's supposed to be the guy to
propose

But I never cared for traditions anyway

If I did, I wouldn't have given it to you on
the first date

And we wouldn't make love until late.

The truth is…

We're meant to each other

Don't fight it, baby

It's not worth it

Just marry me,

It would really piss your mother.

You see baby, you're all I want

You're all I breathe

You're all I need

Just marry me

And let us be.

I know we're broke

And it's not wise

But you can buy me a cheap ring in that
cute little shop

And I'll pretend it's a surprise.

Marry me baby,

I know we're too young

But think it that way:

If we divorce,

We'll still have time to find someone.

Booty Call

You've got it wrong, baby

Cause I don't need you

I don't beg, I don't crawl

If you get hard at night, just use your hand,

Cause I'm not your booty call.

Don't get me wrong,

I like you a little

But I'm so much better than that.

If you want me

Just put a finger on it,

And you better be fast.

Guys like you

I had so many,

But I've got boring of them.

If you like me

Come prove your worth

It's not the other way around.

Call in the morning

And buy me lunch

Maybe that way you'll have a chance.

Cause if you don't,

Don't bother call me at night,

I'm not a booty call.

Me And My Girls

Me and my girls
We are the best
We love each other
We are so blessed.

We take care of each other
We leave no one behind
We don't fuck each other's brothers
Between us, our trust is blind.

They're so hot, smart and strong
I'm so proud of them all the time
Me and my girls, we're unstoppable
Hurt one of them and I'll commit a crime.

Don't be a fool

We have our fights,

But we make up right after it.

Cause there's nothing in this world

That matters more

Than me and my girls.

I Miss Those Rainy Days

We started dating at fifteen

Our bodies knew each other so well

It was with you that I learned everything

The whole school envied what we had.

Your favorite sport was making me come

In your car, on those rainy days

We skipped school to fuck in your home

I miss those rainy days.

Everyone thought we were endgame

I guess I believed that too

I confess: on those rainy days

I used to imagine that I would marry you

I was so naive to believe

That high school sweethearts

Could live happily ever after.

Yes, I know

We were just kids,

But it felt so real, you know?

You always said you wouldn't go to college

And I always said it was my dream

Deep down, I thought I could make you
change your mind

But I was the only one to believe.

The other day I came back to visit

And I was thinking of visiting you

But Mrs. Philips said you'd got married

With three kids and a dog too.

I want you to be happy, I swear
But the idea of you married, made me cry
Maybe I expected you to wait for me
I wasn't ready for goodbye.

Baby, I miss those rainy days.

A Perfect Mess

I'm the mechanic's daughter
The one who fixes your daddy's cars
I remember the first time you saw me
I was smoking one of your cigars.

You yelled at me and called me wild
Made fun of me for being poor
I show you the finger and gave you a smile
And that was it, you were done.

My clothes were always full of oil
Yours impeccably ironed
My hair was always a mess
But I was the only who aroused your desire.

We were a perfect mess, but we were happy
Until your friends found out about me
You were a coward, you didn't fight
You screw it all up, and now I see.

You were too perfect
I was too messy
It would never end up well.
I guess it's a good thing this is over
Now you're dating Chanel.

I'm sure her clothes are always clean
Her hair is perfect all the time,
The only thing I won't forget
Are your perfect nails next to mine.

I see you looking for me in the halls
I don't know why, because we're over

I guess you miss my wild hair,

Spread on the hood of your range rover.

My Brother's Best Friend

We've known each other since forever

You two taught me how to ride a bike

You saw me throw the most annoying
tantrums

That's the problem, you always saw me as a
child.

I always had a crush on you

Always longing for your smile

Everybody knew it, even you

But I was just little Ryle.

Now you finally notice me, I'm seventeen

My boobs had finally grown

You came back from college, a little lost

But now I'm not alone.

I waited for you, but I couldn't wait forever

Someone else came and notice me before you

I can't lie, the crush is still here

But you don't even know what I've been through.

Because it wasn't just a crush, it was true love

But I was just little Ryle to you,

I'm sorry baby, I've moved on

And now, the one with a crush is you.

Fall in love with my brother's best friend

Was always a terrible idea

I couldn't help it, it was love at first sight,

I'm glad it's finally over.

I guess it wasn't meant to be

It was for the best, speaking the truth

Because if we ever had something

My brother would beat the shit out of you.

Daddy's Driver

When I first met you, I was seventeen.

You were just out of school

On that day, I already knew

I would fall in love with you.

You felt the same, I saw it in your eyes

You couldn't keep your hands away

We fucked so much in daddy's car

We had to do it every single day.

You were daddy's driver, but I didn't care

It was too powerful between us,

Two horny teenagers,

You were Mars, I was Venus.

But last night, he found out about us

I guess we were a little reckless,

He fired you and it was a fuss,

About his driver who took advantage of his
little girl.

I already told him; it was not just you

I mean, I was all over you too,

I even remember that day,

I begged you to fuck me on his car's hood.

But he doesn't get it, he thinks I'm a prude

So I'm going with plan B

Tonight around one a.m.

Climb my balcony, use the tree.

I'll be waiting in my bed, legs spread, all
naked,

My room is at the back, so no one will hear
us

It will be worth it, I swear

And after that we'll take the bus.

I'm All Slutty

I'm daddy's little girl

My mother's copy

I'm my grandparents' favorite

But at night, I'm all slutty.

At school, I behave well

I never get off track

Everyone follows me, like they're on some
spell

But at night I'm all slutty.

Being perfect is not easy,

Sometimes I need an escape.

So by day, I'm all nice

But by night, I'm all slutty.

But I kept my nights in secret

Nobody knows where I go

I warned you, at night, I'm all slutty.

I like being fucked, rough and slow.

God, if daddy knew

That his little girl loves to be choked

He would freak out, that's for sure

So only by night, I'm all slut.

Let them think I'm perfect

Let them keep a smile on their faces

They don't need to know I'm fucked every
night

Only by night, I'm all slutty.

Her Name Is Marianne

There's this girl in my class

Everyone knows she's a lesbian

Her eyes look just like glass.

Her name is Marianne.

My boyfriend says she's a freak

No girl comes close to her.

But if you ask me, I'll tell you the truth

At night, I touch myself imagining it's her.

I don't know what's going on with me,

I've been taught to like boys

My boyfriend is cute, I really like him

But he fucks no better than toys.

Yesterday we were in the lock rooms
together
I was nervous, because she was naked.

And for the first time in my life

My arouse wasn't faked.

So I approached her and her body shivered,

I saw goosebumps in her skin,

I touch her breast softly, teased her nipple,

She put her fingers on my clit.

I spread my legs and started moaning,

It was all too much.

She kissed me roughly and I bit her,

It was like I've never been touched.

So, I'm freaking out, because it was great,

My boyfriend never made me feel like that.

So it's safe to say I have a crush

She's beautiful, her name is Marianne.

I Took A Test Yesterday

Baby, I took a test yesterday

And I don't have good news

After I piss on the stick,

a smile appeared on the screen.

I guess we were asking for it

When you came inside me.

But it was just one time

I thought it wouldn't count.

I don't know how I let it happen

At twelve, my mom gave me the talk.

But we were so horny that night

I wish I could go back in time.

Oh baby, this is a mess,

I don't know what we're gonna do

We're too young to be parents

But I go to church, so I will not abort.

We have to figured it out,

Tell our parents is the first thing

I already know my dad will kill me,

Maybe threaten you so you buy me a ring.

Don't worry, it's not what I want

We're too young to get married,

Besides, I'm your best friend's girl,

So let's deal with that when you're ready.

I didn't mean to get pregnant

With my boyfriend's best friend,

But that night you were so sexy,

And you always liked me anyway.

Baby, I Don't Want To Get Married

The ring is beautiful

Your speech was perfect

I have always been faithful

But I don't want to get married

I know we've been dating for years

I know everyone expects this

But I'm not ready yet

Baby, I don't want to get married.

Everyone is looking at us,

Waiting to hear me say YES

Why did you do this in public?

God, this is such a mess.

Why did you have to hurry anyway?
I though we were happy just like this.
There's people here that I don't even know
Maybe if I say no with a kiss?

What do I do? People are gossiping
I'm giving them my best smile
But I already know, they're freaking out
They know I'm about to deny.

But suddenly I have an idea
I think I can get us out of this mess, now
Give me a moment, let me prepare
I'm gonna pretend I'm passing out.

Baby, I don't want to get married.

My Best Friend Is Better Than Yours

I have a best friend,

We've known each other since forever

Sometimes we fight like enemies,

Sometimes we sleep naked.

We're used to share everything

It's us against the world

We share food, beds and make-up,

We share books, boys and clothes.

We always share all the boys,

To talk about the experience later,

But sometimes the boys bore us

On those nights, we sleep naked.

My best friend is better than yours
She knows my body better than anyone,
Sometimes at night in my bed,
She touches my tits and kisses my cunt.

Nobody knows our night activities,
Nobody knows our connection.
The way I pinch her nipples,
And in return, she makes me come in seconds.

Baby, You're So Gay

Baby, you're so gay

Why do you try to hide it?

Everyone knows, it's in your face,

So I don't know why you try to get inside
me.

It's for the show, right?

It has to be.

You're lying to everyone.

But it's you who's been lied to.

People don't care

It's the twenty-first century

Do what you want

I know you like Emory.

Why are you wasting time

Worrying about other people's thoughts?

They're your friends and if they ghost you

It will only be their loss.

Baby, you're so gay,

Just go live your life.

Just be brave and get what you want

Because you'll never be happy with a wife.

It Was Your Loss Baby, Not Mine

It was your loss baby, not mine,

I was the best girlfriend in the world

I would cook for you and then suck you,

I wish I used my teeth one of those times.

But like all boys, you were deceived,

You thought you could make better than
me,

Poor baby, you were so fooled,

She's bad at giving head, everyone can see.

But I guess you'll find out by yourself

And when you do, I'm gonna be the one
who laughs

Poor baby, you were so fooled,

It was only your loss, not mine.

You will come back crawling, I know it

Asking me to take you back.

But I've moved on too, I'm not dumb,

Right now, I'm fucking your friend Jack.

I Shouldn't Be Fucking My Stepbrother

Our parents don't know

That we sneak out sometimes

It's not our fault

That our parents married each other.

This shouldn't be happening,

But it's not like we can control it,

Your room is just next to mine

And I've been really lonely.

The angst is always there

The air is too heavy

They can't forbid us, it wouldn't be fair

They shouldn't have married.

Any corner of the house, you're always
there

You are always on top of me,

And when our parents aren't home,

You make me come until I count three.

We sleep together every night

We can't take our hands off each other,

Our parents can never know,

I shouldn't be fucking my stepbrother.

Can I Just Be Your Daughter?

Stop pressuring me

It's exhausting.

I'll never be who you want me to.

Your expectations are becoming dauting.

I don't want to be a doctor

I don't want to be a lawyer

I don't want to be a teacher

Can I just be your daughter?

I know you wanted me to think big,

I know you're not proud of me.

But try to see my side: it's my life,

Can I just be your daughter?

In our family everyone goes to college,

And I was supposed to follow suit.

But what if we break tradition?

What if I want to sell fruit?

Really, you have to get over it.

Cause I'm not going to college.

Don't worry, you have two more kids,

I'm sure you'll win them over.

Daddy, can I just be your daughter?

I'm really happy the way I am.

I want to make my own choices.

So don't force me, or I'll run.

My Boyfriend's Brother

It was a warm and calm night
I was crashing at my boyfriend's home
I went downstairs to drink some water,
I barely had clothes on.

I was drinking a glass of water
When I noticed a dark figure
You were there in silence
And the air became thicker.

Your gaze was lock on my naked body
And mine was in your muscled chest,
We talked for hours, you had questions
And you really made me laugh.

After some time, the tension tightened,
We were alone and we both wanted it
You kissed me first and I startled,
But then your brother woke up.

Since that night, everything has changed
And sometimes we sneak out.
Your brother doesn't know,
That you've been fucking my brains out.

I know it's wrong, we should not do this,
And we always swear it's the last time,
But then the air thickens again,
I just hope he doesn't find.

My boyfriend's brother is off limits
That's what I should've thought
But now I am addicted,

So we're doing it until we get caught.

You Are The Key

Whenever I'm sad I end up at your door

Wondering where you are,

You are the key baby

You were always the key.

I wish I could knock

I wish I could come in

I wish I was still yours

And you could end this sadness.

I'm hurting so bad,

Cause I can't get over the fact

I won't see you again.

I tell myself this is the last time

I'm coming here

But then my heart hurts and I need the key

And baby you're the key.

It's embarrassing, really,

This is not even your home anymore

The new owners keep staring me,

They probably think I'm a moron.

I wish this was still your house,

At least I could come in,

I would hug your mother and talk to her for
hours,

Because you had her eyes.

It hurts so bad, baby,

You were the only key.

What do I do now?

Why did you leave?

I know it's not your fault,
But sometimes, when I'm really bad,
I blame you
You shouldn't have gone to that party,
You shouldn't have got in that car.

Now, I'm here and no key,
There's no way for the pain to end.
I'll just keep coming to your old house,
I wish you weren't dead.

Just a Bunch Of Crazy People

Sometimes I look around

And I don't recognize anyone

Who is this people?

Where did common sense go?

Teenagers are pretending to be adults,

Adults are working like crazy,

Children are being forgotten,

Old people are dying, and no one is caring.

The world looks faker than ever,

I don't know what we're doing.

We run after the wrong things,

And we only regret when we're eighty.

Am I just like them?

Just a bunch of crazy people?

There's no one putting an end on this?

Seriously, what are we doing?

We're fighting for the wrong things,

We're chasing the wrong people,

We're working for the wrong reasons,

We're just a bunch of crazy people.

I'm Not Going To Break

I'm not going to break

I'm not in denial

Everybody treats me like porcelain

When I keep saying that everything is fine.

People die every day,

I'm not the only one graving

I just need time to make everything better

Otherwise, I'll just be faking.

I'm not going to break

I have everything under control

When I'm almost in tears, I swallow them

Then I put a smile and I move on.

I just miss him, you know?

I remember that day on the lake

We talked, we laugh, we fought.

But I swear I'm not going to break.

When it becomes too much, I drink

There's a scotch bottle in my dad's closet.

It's almost empty, I drank it all.

But I swear I'm not going to break.

You're Not Gonna Change, Are You?

Everyone told me that you weren't going to
change

But I thought I was smarter than them

Now I'm hurting because I was wrong

You're not going to change, are you?

I always knew you were a player

But I wanted to believe that you would
change,

God, I believed I was it for you,

But you're not going to change, are you?

Why would you change for me

When you can have a different girl every
night?

You were never a one-woman man

And I only realized it tonight.

I blame your mother,

She made you believe that you could have
everything you want.

But she was wrong about one thing,

You don't have me anymore.

You're not going to change, are you?

I'm Not Selfish When I'm With You

My daddy always told me

That I could have everything I wanted

I truly believed it

And I lived my life like that.

What I wanted, I had,

What I didn't have, I demanded,

People didn't bother me

They knew it wasn't a good idea.

But then I laid eyes on you,

And you were different from everyone else,

You didn't fall for my bullshit,

And that was what started this mess.

The problem was: you didn't let me have
you,

So I did what I was used to

I made plans and demanded what I wanted.

But that would never work with you.

You called me spoiled, grumpy and selfish,

And it really bothered me at first.

For the first time in my life,

I realized that my dad had spoiled me.

So I realize I had to change,

That I couldn't be selfish with you,

I grew up, I become a woman,

I became someone worthy of you.

DEAR READER

Thank you for reading *I'm not a good girl* from the series "Good Girls Write Poetry".

I hope you loved it as much as I loved writing it!

Also, follow me on Instagram @aurorajuneauthor so you can know more about me and my other books.

Aurora